WAY

Sally Hewitt

W
FRANKLIN WATTS
LONDON · SYDNEY

This edition 2006
First published in 2004 by
Franklin Watts
338 Euston Road
London NW1 3BH

Franklin Watts Australia
Hachette Children's Books
Level 17/207 Kent Street
Sydney, NSW 2000

© Franklin Watts 2004

ISBN-10: 0-7496-5578-X
ISBN-13: 978-0-5578-5

Series editor: Sally Luck
Art director: Jonathan Hair
Design: Rachel Hamdi/Holly Mann
Picture Research: Diana Morris

A CIP catalogue record for this book is available
from the British Library.

Every attempt has been made to clear copyright. Should there
be any inadvertent omission, please apply to
the publisher for rectification.

Printed in China

Franklin Watts is a division of Hachette Children's Books.

Contents

What is a holiday?

A holiday is time off school or work. It is time to have a rest, an adventure or to go somewhere new.

There are three long school holidays in a year.

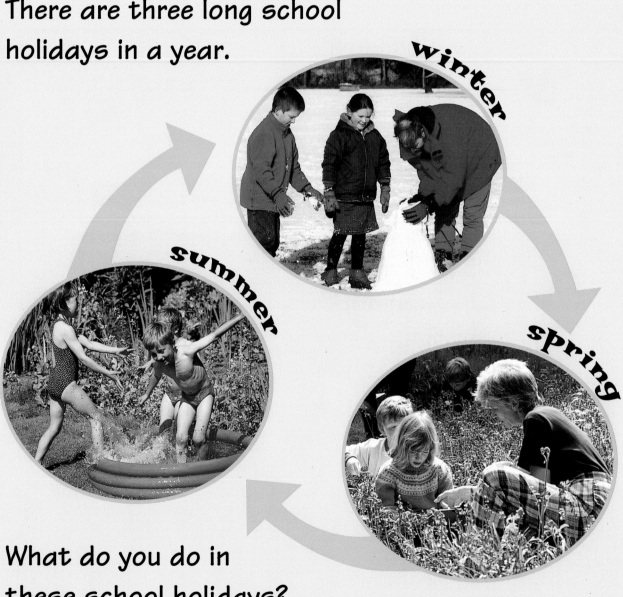

winter

summer

spring

What do you do in these school holidays?
Which holidays include religous festivals?

The school summer holiday is often the longest holiday of the year. The weather is warm so people like to go to the seaside.

💬 Talk about...

... why summer is a good time for a long holiday. Use these words to help you:

long days   sunshine   hot

outdoors   swim   walk

Postcards

People travel all over the world to go on holiday and do exciting things.

Some people send postcards back home. Have you ever sent a postcard? What did you write?

Dear Gran

The sun shines every day. I swam with a dolphin!

love from
Sam

x x x

Mrs Webster

3 Pond Street

Newcastle Upon Tyne

NE27 1BU

Three children are packing to go on holiday. Where do you think they are going? Match what they are taking to the postcards on page 8.

Have you been on holiday? Where did you go? What did you do?

G tting th re!

Today we can travel all over the world in aeroplanes, trains, boats and cars.

🔍 Be a historian...

In Victorian times, 150 years ago, these modern forms of transport did not exist. Victorians travelled by steam train. Where do you think they went on holiday?

Victorian families went on holiday to the seaside! Have you been to any of these seaside resorts?

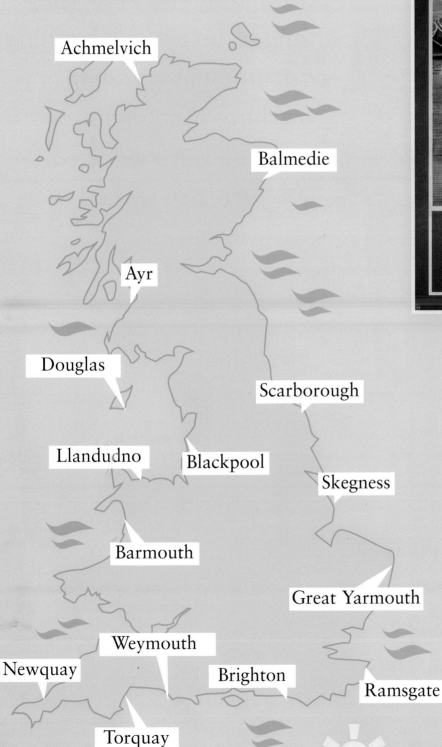

Achmelvich

Balmedie

Ayr

Douglas

Scarborough

Llandudno   Blackpool

Skegness

Barmouth

Great Yarmouth

Weymouth

Newquay   Brighton

Ramsgate

Torquay

△ Steam trains took people to the seaside until the 1960s. This poster is from 1930.

What do you think the Victorians did at the seaside? Turn the page to find out...

Victorian seaside

At the seaside, people paddled in the sea. They changed into their bathing costumes in wooden bathing machines. These were wheeled into the water!

△ Victorian bathing machines and bathing costumes ▷

Be a historian...

Why do you think the machines were wheeled into the sea? What would it feel like to swim in a Victorian bathing costume?

Children paddled and built sandcastles, just like they do today. Compare this picture to the one on page 7. What is different? What is the same?

△ Victorian children playing at the seaside

Talk about...

... what it was like on a Victorian beach.

Use these words to help you:

| bathing machines | wheels | paddling |
| buckets and spades | crowds | bathing costumes |

Seaside attractions

Most seaside towns have a promenade where you can stroll. One hundred years ago, people sat and listened to brass bands.

Band playing on the promenade ▷

Oh, I do like to be
Beside the seaside,
Oh I do like to be
Beside the sea,
Oh I do like to stroll
Upon the
Prom, Prom, Prom,
Where the brass bands play
Tiddely-om-pom-pom!

◁ English music hall song, written and composed in 1907

Have you heard anyone singing this song?
Have you heard a brass band play?
What do you think brass bands sound like?

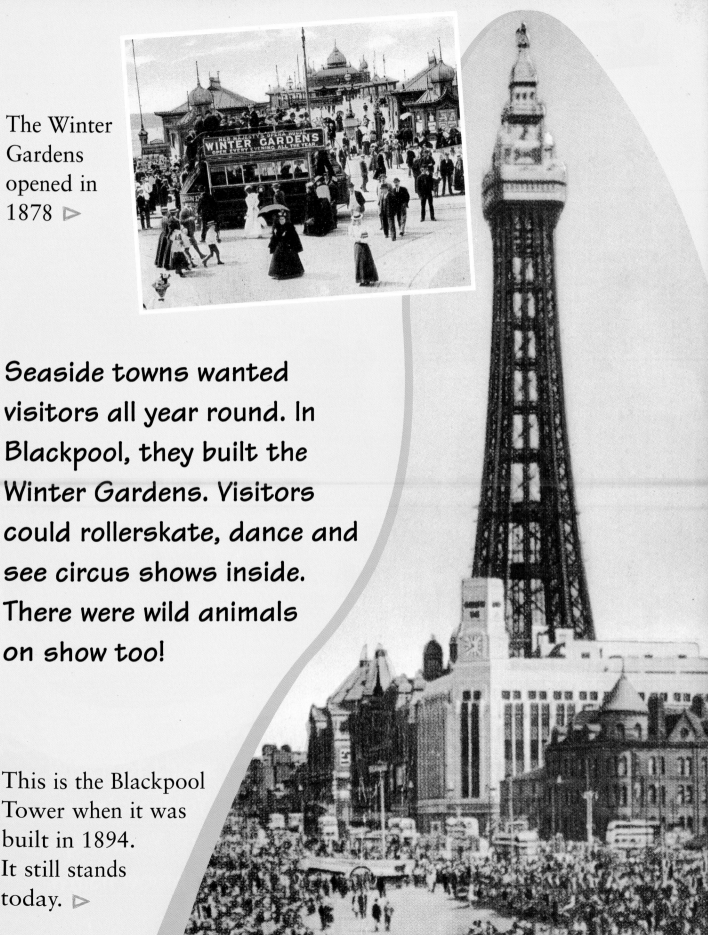

The Winter Gardens opened in 1878 ▷

Seaside towns wanted visitors all year round. In Blackpool, they built the Winter Gardens. Visitors could rollerskate, dance and see circus shows inside. There were wild animals on show too!

This is the Blackpool Tower when it was built in 1894. It still stands today. ▷

The 1940s and 1950s

△ The seafront, during the war

In the 1940s, World War II took place. Many beaches were closed. Barbed wire fences were put up to help stop the enemy invading. Mines were buried under the sand.

A wartime poster ▷

Not these shells..

... but THESE

"STAY PUT" THIS SUMMER
In peace-time the Railways welcome holiday crowds.
This summer holidays should be spent
at home.
RAILWAY EXECUTIVE COMMITTEE

Be a historian...

Look at the poster.

What are the two types of shell?

How does the poster make you feel?

Do you think it helped stop people from going to the beach?

In the 1950s, when war was over, the beaches re-opened. Families were glad to be able to go on holiday again.

Crowded beach in the 1950s ▽

Ask your grandparents to tell you about trips to the seaside when they were young.

The 1960s and 1970s

In the 1960s and 1970s, fashion went wild! Everyone wanted the latest beach wear that they saw in magazines.

Magazine adverts from the 1960s

Silhouette *sunsoakers*
make some pretty patterns on the beach.

Two styles~S661 and S662~of the Silhouette range. Photographed in Martinique.

Talk about...

... the beach wear in these adverts.
Use these words to help you:
fashion   patterns   colourful   bright   bold

Children wore nylon swimsuits that dried quickly in the sun. They played with beach balls and airbeds called lilos.

🔍 Be a historian...

Look back at page 13.
How have things changed for children at the seaside since then?
Ask your parents what it was like at the seaside when they were young.

Seaside fun

At the seaside, we build sandcastles, collect shells and paddle. Sometimes we ride a donkey or watch a Punch and Judy show, just like Victorian children did!

△ Punch and Judy show, 100 years ago

◁ Punch and Judy show today

The Punch and Judy show never changes. The crocodile always eats the sausages!

Have you ever seen a Punch and Judy show?

22

Donkeys with names like Neddy, Raffles and Gloria take children for rides along the sands. In the winter, they get a long rest.

◁ Donkey rides in the past

Donkey rides today ▷

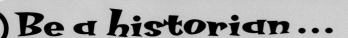

🔍 Be a historian…

Why do you think children do the same things on the beach as they did a long time ago?

What do holidaymakers do in the sea today? Turn the page to find out…

In the sea

One hundred years ago, not many people could swim. They paddled in shallow water.

Today, people enjoy all kinds of water sports.

⬤ Talk about...

... what these people are doing.
Use these words to help you:

water sports

canoeing

surfing

jet-skiing

🔍 Be a historian...

Look back through the book and find ways in which
seaside holidays have changed.
How are they still the same?

Souvenirs

A souvenir is something to take home to remind you of your holiday. It can cheer you up on a cold winter's day!

Be a historian...

What tells you these souvenirs are from the seaside?
Which do you think is the oldest souvenir? Can you say why?

People who travel around the world bring back souvenirs from wonderful places.

△ T-shirt from the United States

Drums from ▷ North Africa

△ A mask from Cuba

Have you brought back a souvenir from a holiday abroad? Do you have any souvenirs of the seaside?

27

Timeline

Start

1837 – 1901
Victorian Britain
Seaside holidays
become popular.

1840s
Steam trains
take people
to seaside
resorts.

1894
The Blackpool Tower is built.

1907
The popular song
"Oh I do like to be
beside the seaside"
is written.

**World War II
1939 – 1945**
Beaches fenced off
with barbed wire to
help stop the enemy
invading.

1950s
Beaches are re-opened
and are crowded with
holidaymakers.

1960s
Travelling abroad by
aeroplane becomes
cheaper.

1970s – Today
Water sports, such as
surfing and jet-skiing
become popular.

Today
More people go on
holiday abroad than
ever before!

End

Glossary

Bathing machine
Wooden huts where Victorian bathers changed into bathing costumes. They could be wheeled into the sea.

Coast
The place where land meets sea.

Dock
To tie a boat up to land. A dock is also a place where boats are tied up.

Pier
A platform built out to sea, where boats can dock and people can walk and fish.

Promenade
A walkway along the seashore.

Seaside resort
A place on the coast where holidaymakers go for a seaside holiday.

Souvenir
Something you take home to remind you of your holiday.

Steam train
Steam trains are powered by steam engines and use coal for fuel. Today trains are powered by diesel or electricity.

Index